AN UNSPOKEN
BROKEN

AN UNSPOKEN
BROKEN

*Walking Through
The pain of a miscarriage*

AMY LISZKIEWICZ

XULON PRESS

Xulon Press
2301 Lucien Way #415
Maitland, FL 32751
407.339.4217
www.xulonpress.com

Unless otherwise indicated, Scripture quotations taken
from the Holy Bible, New International Version (NIV).
Copyright © 1973, 1978, 1984, 2011 by Biblica, Inc.™.
Used by permission. All rights reserved.

Printed in the United States of America.

ISBN-13: 978-1-66280-546-2

For my two babies that I will one day meet in Glory, and for my husband Christopher who always supported my dream.

TABLE OF CONTENTS

A NOTE TO
THE READER...

I WANT TO START OFF BY SAYING THAT IN this book I bare my soul to you. I will tell you of my story and how I found healing. My story is one of deep pain, extreme emotional struggle, and the unending love of God. It is only by the prompting and grace of God that I have been able to write this book, and I pray that it touches your heart in some way.

The very first thing you need to know is that you are not alone and you are prayed for. I don't know you, but I am covering you in prayer as I write this book. From one heart to another... you are not alone. I am assuming that you are reading this book because you or someone you are close to has had to walk through the immense pain of losing a child because of a miscarriage. You are not alone. I am in no way an expert on this subject, but I have found that many times our culture is very silent about this surprisingly common occurrence. You are not alone. I am not a professional writer, but an ordinary woman that felt God was calling her to share her story with those that need comfort and encouragement. You are not alone.

Are you catching the repetition? You are not alone. When walking through a miscarriage one of the hardest things is the feeling of loneliness. Your husband may be there and be very supportive, but he doesn't truly understand the depth of your pain, and if you are anything like me, I was afraid to tell anyone. I didn't want people to know about my miscarriage and offer me some well-meaning but hurtful advice like, "well at least the baby wasn't born yet" or "you can always try again…" I have learned; however, that I needed to share my pain in order to heal. I needed to speak up about this common heartache so that others felt free to do the same and begin to get the support and healing they needed. I pray that this book will help you work through your loss. I pray that you know that you are not alone. I pray that you know that your Heavenly Father sees you, right now, in this moment. He wants you to run to Him for comfort. He longs to have you turn to Him instead of away from Him.

I pray that your healing begins…

PART I

MY STORY

I AM A PERSON THAT LIKES CONTROL. I like my "ducks in a row," and I like to know what to expect at any given moment. I am a planner, and when things do not go according to my plan I feel completely out of control. When I was younger I knew I was going to be a teacher by the time I was in fifth grade. I knew what college I wanted to go to by the time I was in middle school, and I wanted to be married shortly after I graduated from college.

God graciously allowed all of those things to take place in my life. I loved the idea of planning out my life and having everything go according to my plan, to my timetable, just the way I wanted it to. I started to think that I had control over my life. I could not have been more wrong.

God was about to walk my husband and I through some very difficult circumstances. As a planner, my husband and I planned out that we were going to wait for two years to start a family. We had some student loans to pay off and we wanted to make sure we had time to adjust as a married couple before we welcomed our little ones into this world.

A year and a half went by, and I had to have an emergency surgery to remove my appendix. It was totally unexpected and unplanned. As a result of a high deductible insurance plan, we now had some medical bills that needed to be paid off. While away on our two year anniversary trip, my husband sat down with me and asked if we could wait one more year to have children. I hesitantly agreed. My heart ached for a child, but I needed to submit to my husband. I knew that he wanted children just as badly, but he wanted to make sure we were ready financially.

The following year flew by faster than I had dared hope, and we were finally ready to start a family. I was pregnant within a month of trying. I went to the store and bought those foam letters kids use in the bathtub and spelled out "We're Pregnant" on the wall of our shower to let my husband know. He was so excited he rushed upstairs and hugged me. We were elated. I had a blood test a few days later to confirm the pregnancy, and my doctor told me to set up an appointment for my first ultrasound.

After scheduling the ultrasound for four weeks later, it really began to sink in that we were going to have a baby. I was going to be able to see my baby laugh and giggle. I was going to hold my baby and rock him or her to sleep. I couldn't wait.

The ultrasound never came.

A few weeks after my blood test, I started to bleed and immediately called my doctor. She said to stay off my feet and give it some time to see what happens. I remember sitting on my bed talking on the phone to my grandma. She was talking to me about a chair that my great uncle was getting rid of and wanted to know if Christopher and I wanted it. It's funny the little details you remember when you go through a traumatic event. As I sat on the bed talking with her I felt severe cramps coming and going. I told her I had to go and then walked around trying to alleviate the pain. I continued to bleed.

Our church does an event called Clue Night where people dress up as different characters and the visitors come around and try to solve a puzzle using clues. I remember a day or two after the initial bleeding started, helping my husband set up his area for the event. He kept telling me to take it easy, but I already knew it didn't matter. I was losing the baby and there was nothing that could be done. The cramping and bleeding did not stop until my baby was gone. It was my first miscarriage. The joy had been stripped from my heart almost as soon as I had gotten it. I went from daydreaming about my precious little one to extreme emotional and physical pain.

Several weeks after I miscarried my parents had a party at their house and Christopher and I went. While mingling with the people at the party a woman, in front of my mom and several other ladies, asked me if Christopher and I were going to try to have kids soon. I answered with "when God blesses us with children we will have them." The woman then said, "Ahh, so you must be trying then… good for you!" I wanted to do nothing more than run and hide. I wanted to scream at her that we had a baby, but the baby died. I was pregnant a few weeks ago, but God took my baby away. Instead, I just smiled weakly and quietly walked away. My heart was so utterly broken.

My doctor offered her sympathies, but she also explained to us that it is more common than many people think to lose your first baby because your body has not adjusted to what it is like to carry a baby yet. Although my husband and I were devastated we were also ready to try again, and soon after, I was pregnant again in January. We were so thankful that we did not have problems with being able to get pregnant, and we were so hopeful that this time we would finally welcome our baby into this world. Everything seemed to be going great. My blood test came back positive, my levels all looked great, I didn't have any signs of bleeding, and I was scheduled for my first ultrasound at 7 ½ weeks. I allowed myself to hope. I believed that this was going to work out. I began to dream again of that precious little one in my arms. I was really excited because we were leaving in a little over a week to go on Easter break with my family to Florida, and I was going to share the picture of the ultrasound with them. I pictured in my head what that fun reveal to our family would be like. The one where you take the pictures of the ultrasound, frame them, and wrap them up and give them to all the grandparents, aunt, uncles, etc. Then they open the little boxes at the same time and get so excited about this new little addition to the family. I was so excited for that reveal that every new mom dreams about…I was so excited.

I very foolishly went to the appointment by myself, totally not anticipating anything would be wrong. Why would it be? The doctor had told us that the first miscarriage was a result of it simply being my first pregnancy, and my hormone levels were picture perfect for this pregnancy.

When I was in the ultrasound room during my appointment the woman doing the procedure was very quiet and eventually brought in another woman to help her. I started to get the feeling that something was very wrong. Both of the women were too quiet, and they kept avoiding eye contact. My head was telling me that something was not right, but my heart refused to accept that anything was amiss.

After about an hour of them checking things out they informed me that the baby had no heartbeat. I think I must have simply given them a blank stare at first, because they had to repeat it to me several times. When what they were trying to communicate to me finally sunk in, I immediately broke down and sobbed. Not a little sob or sniffle because I'm crying sob... an uncontrollable sob. It was an out of control sob. Looking back I most likely made both of those women extremely uncomfortable, but they graciously gave me some tissues and gave me some space. This could not be happening. Not again. They told me that I needed to come back in a week to see if the baby had grown and developed a heartbeat. The baby was measuring just under what the maximum size is in order to make the call for a nonviable pregnancy when there is no heartbeat. The doctors told me to come back, but that it did not look good.

I rode home that day in utter shock. I was in disbelief and scared to death. When I got home my husband met me at the door with a smile on his face. He was obviously excited to see the ultrasound pictures that we were going to share with our family on vacation. When he looked at my face his smile quickly vanished. I just shook my head no and started to sob. I had to tell my husband that once again we may lose a baby. That all that pain and heartache was knocking at our door once again. I had to tell him that my body has once again failed him in providing a child. The only hope I clung to was that maybe the baby would have a heartbeat at the following appointment in a week.

That week was the longest week of my life. I was never a very patient person, and this was amplified by intense emotion and fear. Every waking moment I prayed and cried out to God to allow my child to have a heartbeat when I went back in for my next appointment. I had a lot of waking moments. I don't think I slept more than a few hours each night. I was overwhelmed with fear and anxiety. I tried to keep myself busy. I tried not to think about it. I tried not to burst into tears every time I looked into the eyes of one of my fifth grade students at school and longed to one day have a child of my own, and fearing that the one inside of me would not make it.

During that week I was bombarded not only with the inner turmoil, but the comments that come from people when you are at a certain age and married. One night that week Christopher and I were at youth groups because we work with the teens, and one of the other youth leaders was talking with me and mentioned that someday I would have a ton of babysitters for my kids. It was such an innocent comment, but it broke my heart. Little did they know that I was currently begging God for the life of my child.

Another incident occurred when a person made a comment to me about snacking and hinting that I might be eating for two. They even threw in a wink with the comment. I simply gave them a death stare and walked away. It was probably not the Godliest response, but it was all I could do in the moment. I was carrying a child inside me, but I didn't know if I was ever going to meet them this side of heaven. Not to mention that even if I was not pregnant and going through a tough time, the comment was totally uncalled for. Sometimes people just have what I call "diarrhea of the mouth." As you read this, I beg you to please, never be one of those people. If you find yourself on the receiving end; however, remember that God's grace is sufficient. I did not always react the way I should have, but I tried to keep in mind that none of these people knew what I was walking through. They were not trying to be cruel or mean, and I needed to keep that in perspective.

A week later, my husband and I went in and had the second ultrasound. I tried to put on a brave face, and my husband tried to keep the subjects of conversation light. We were both terrified, but were not allowing ourselves to express the fear we felt. The woman came in and started the procedure. All the while my husband and I talked about work and other mundane topics.

When she was finished she led us to a waiting area and told us to wait for the doctor to see us. We both knew what was coming, but we were still in denial. We both refused to vocalize what we already knew. The doctor opened the door to his office and called us into a room with a bunch of computer screens. He pulled up our ultrasound images. I saw our precious baby on that screen as he told us that it was a nonviable pregnancy and that our baby would not survive. I very calmly asked him if the ultrasound technician could have made a mistake. He continued to explain to us that it was very cut and dry that the baby would not make it. There was no growth present, still no heartbeat, and the baby would not survive. I would have to walk through a second miscarriage.

The doctor told me that I needed to speak with my OBGYN to discuss what steps now needed to be taken. He told me that because this was my second nonviable pregnancy that I should not pursue any more pregnancies until I had some testing done. As we walked out of his office, I allowed the first floods of emotion to hit me. I tried to keep it together until I could reach the car, but as we were walking out I started to sob. The sobs wracked my whole body. My husband literally had to hold me up as we walked out to the car. I was numb and felt as though I could not breathe. This could not be happening again.

My husband had met me at the radiology place because I had gone straight from work. This meant I had to drive home. I had to stop crying enough to actually see the road and make rational driving decisions. I remember my husband wrapping his arms around me in the parking lot and whispering to me that one day it would happen, that one day we would hold our own baby. I was doubtful. I was so full of loss and grief that I was numb. I was thinking *yeah right, it's never going to happen, Amy, just get over it.* His hug and my sudden yet temporary apathy was enough to get me in the car to drive myself home. While driving, I remember my husband driving up next to me at signals and making silly faces at me. He was doing anything to keep my focus off of what had just happened, and I love him deeply for that. He was amazing at knowing just what I needed in the moment to simply survive. That night was the first of many that I sobbed myself to sleep.

My OBGYN called me shortly after the ultrasound and told me that I had two choices with my nonviable pregnancy. I could wait for up to five weeks and allow my body to miscarry naturally or I could have a D&C. When my doctor described a D&C to me as a procedure that is used for abortions, and even though my baby was no longer alive, I could not mentally come to grips with doing it and decided to wait for my body to miscarry naturally. Please understand that I do not judge anyone who has had a D&C because their baby was no longer alive. There is nothing wrong with having one to remove a nonviable pregnancy. The baby was not alive, but for me, I just couldn't do it. It took almost a full five weeks before I started to bleed. Five weeks of feeling and looking pregnant, and yet knowing the child I carried was dead inside of me.

I remember a specific incident during those five weeks that totally wrecked me. A colleague told me that he overheard some of my students talking during gym class about how they thought I was pregnant. During those five weeks my body had still not recognized that the pregnancy was nonviable and so I continued to grow and look like I might be pregnant. When I heard his comment, which he made in front of everyone in the break room at the time, I felt like shouting… I am pregnant… but my baby is dead so leave me alone. Why would someone say something like that to me? Why would anyone insinuate that a woman is pregnant when they don't really know? I was angry and hurt beyond words. This too was another moment where God's grace had to step in. Although the words he chose to speak were not the wisest, he was not intentionally trying to hurt me.

Once I started to bleed I was given pills to take on the weekend to expedite the miscarriage. I picked up the pills on a Friday because it only makes sense that if I was going to have to go through this I should do it over a weekend so that I wouldn't miss as much work. That night Christopher and I went to his parents' house to play some games and have dinner. The whole time I was thinking *tonight is the night, tonight I will truly lose my baby.* After a while, I told Christopher that we needed to get going. On the way home I filled him in on what the doctor said to expect after I took the pills. When we got home I took two of these small round pills, trudged upstairs, and tried in vain to get some sleep.

The pain started around 2 a.m. It was an extremely intense, cramping pain. Essentially my body was having contractions. I got up out of bed and paced the floor in the upstairs of our apartment trying to move around to alleviate some of the pain. After half an hour or so the pain was only intensifying so I decided to go downstairs and take a warm bath to again try to ease the pain. I remember just sitting in the water with tears streaming down my face. My husband was fast asleep as I lay utterly alone in a tub of water in deep emotional and physical pain. After a while the water got cold and I drained it out. As I stood to get up out of the tub the first gush of blood and tissue came. I was shocked and started to sob and weep loudly. I'm not sure if I actually screamed or just cried out, but my husband was there in a matter of seconds. We both just stared at all the blood and tissue in the tub. I looked up at him with the deepest pain in my eyes as he asked if I was ok. I was not ok. I felt as if I was never going to be ok. I replied that I was ok; however, and said that this is what the doctor said to expect. Another wave of pain came over me at that moment.

Not to get too graphic, but I will tell you that there was so much blood and tissue that my husband wanted to call 911, and I had to keep reassuring him that this is what was supposed to happen. At one point I was throwing up in the toilet because of the pain, and the pressure from throwing up caused more blood and tissue to gush onto the floor. I have never seen more blood in real life than I did that night. I had just lost my second baby. No one should have to go through that. It is not only physically painful and scary, it is emotionally unbearable. Once the pain subsided we had to clean up the mess. I had to use paper towels and water to "wipe up" my dead baby and all the blood and other tissue. I threw all those bloodied paper towels into the trash and put on a pad because there was still bleeding although not as heavy. My husband had me lay on the couch because it was downstairs and closer to the bathroom if I should need to get there quickly at any point during the rest of the night. We put some opened trash bags on the couch and covered them in blankets so that my bleeding wouldn't ruin the couch. Again, I laid down and cried myself to sleep for the um-teenth time in the past few months.

The next morning I was very drained both mentally and physically. I was on auto-pilot. I was a shell of a person that was half dead inside, or at least so it felt. Later that day I went to throw something out and I freaked. When I opened the trash can I saw all of the blood from the previous night. I again started to sob and asked my husband if he would take out the garbage immediately. It was the first of many very painful reminders in the weeks to come that I had lost another child. My heart felt not as if it had broken in two, but as if someone had taken a sledge hammer to it and smashed it to smithereens. This all took place the weekend before Mother's Day…

Being the head of the Women's ministry at my church means that part of my job description is putting on the Mother's Day brunch every year, and so I stood, a week after losing my second child, introducing the speaker and talking about how great moms are. All the while, I was thinking, *God, how can this be happening? How can you ask me to do this? How am I supposed to run a Mother's Day brunch when I have just lost yet another baby?* I will tell you that it was only by the grace of God that I was able to stand before those women and get through that day.

There were so many other moments that hurt so deeply. I remember at church that Sunday morning … one week after losing my baby and they played a cute video on the screen about how amazing moms are. My tears were not tears of joy at watching the cute kids playing with their mom, mine were of deep sorrow and pain over what I had lost. On the way out of church they were passing out chocolate to all of the moms and one of the gentlemen passing out chocolate said… "Don't worry… your time will come soon…" Oh, how I wish he would have known…how I wish he would have kept his mouth quiet. There were well-meaning people, but with such few words, they became so unknowingly hurtful. I remember one of my colleagues asking me if working with kids all day made me want some of my own. If only she had known…

Even a week after I miscarried I was still bleeding about the amount of a normal period, but it was starting to subside. My class of fifth graders and I were going to go on our field trip to Gettysburg for three days. The first night there I passed another large clot. Another sharp and painful reminder that I had lost a child just a week and a half ago. I was concerned that I may have some issues with pain and would be unable to lead a three day field trip that entailed a lot of walking around. I contemplated telling the dad on our trip that was also a doctor about what was going on. I wanted someone to know that if I passed out while walking around all day that it may be because of all the blood I had lost, but I decided against it. I still wasn't ready to talk about it with anyone other than my husband. I kept it to myself and mustered through a trip with crazy fifth graders and parents that asked me at dinner when I think I might have kids of my own. Yet again, God's grace had to step in and help me overcome more emotional pain.

I remember another couple in our church walking through a miscarriage at the same time as us. They had just announced on Facebook that they were pregnant and found out within a day or two that their baby was no longer alive. My heart broke for them. Their loss was also so real and deep, and I remember everyone at church talking non-stop about it. As the church gossip and chatter continued, all I wanted to do is tell them that I didn't want to talk about it because I was barely holding it together... but of course, they didn't know what I was going through. They had no idea that I too was walking through a painful loss. I remember family members and friends of the family, although well meaning, constantly asking me when Christopher and I were going to have children. I remember a friend of mine coming to visit and being very pregnant. She went on and on about how excited she was and how cool it was to feel the baby move. Don't get me wrong, I was excited for her, but in that moment, I was finding it hard to "rejoice with those who rejoice..." A verse I never even fathomed would be so hard to live out.

The pain both emotionally and physically, as well as the spiritual confusion and doubt that comes with a miscarriage is real and it is deep. I tell people that I wouldn't wish the experience of this on anyone, not even my worst enemy. Unless you walk through it you cannot fully comprehend what it is like. The emotions that you experience are overwhelming and all-consuming.

PART II

EMOTIONS

BEFORE I DIVE INTO THE EMOTIONAL side of miscarriage, I want to take just a brief moment to look at the physical aspects. When going through a miscarriage, within the midst of it, there is a deep physical pain that is only exacerbated by emotional misery. During a miscarriage, your body, for all intents and purposes is going through labor, but at the end of the pain there is no reward, no precious baby to hold, and no joy. At the end of this kind of labor, there is only more pain and deep sadness caused by an unspeakable loss. A loss that we feel within the very depths of our soul. A loss that no one should have to experience, but a loss that is so very common in our world.

From a medical standpoint, when a woman experiences the loss of a pregnancy, hormone levels are all over the place. There are so many different hormones involved in pregnancy, and when the baby is no longer within the mother, those levels all drop very quickly. This sudden change in hormone levels is what can create an even more intense emotional state. That being said, the emotions I felt, and I am about to walk you though were very real, very intense, and also very exacerbated by the physical drop of pregnancy hormones. The hormones do not mean that the emotional pain was not real, it just means that the emotions are intensified by the physical circumstances. It is similar to when a woman has her menstrual cycle. I don't know about you, but when I am having my "time of the month," I am more lethargic and irritable. This doesn't mean; however, that my neighbor's loud music isn't annoying, it just means that the amount to which it annoys me is more when I am experiencing my period. The same is true with a miscarriage. The emotional pain is still very real, but it is intensified by a woman's hormone levels. This can create a "perfect storm" so to speak of depression and anger.

So many emotions come along with a miscarriage, and every woman is most likely very different in the order in which they feel these emotions and how intensely they feel each one. I simply want to share my journey in hopes of comforting those of you who have walked this road. I want you to know that you are not alone, and to validate your feelings and emotions. I also want to show you that God's grace is greater. It is greater than all our pain and anger.

I remember after that first ultrasound telling myself that everything would be fine when I went back in a week, but deep down, I had this feeling that I was very wrong. I prayed that week like I have never prayed before. I felt like Hannah from the Bible. Hannah prayed for a son, and she was so overcome by emotion that Eli the priest thought she was drunk. I remember crying out to God, begging Him to save my baby and allow him or her to have a heartbeat when I went back in a week. So when the doctor told us a week later that the baby would not make it…the first two emotions reared their ugly heads. Anger and denial flooded my heart.

I told you that I questioned the doctor and asked him if there was any way that they could have made a mistake. That was only the beginning of my denial. Deep down, of course, I knew the truth, but I tried to cling to any hope. Just days after I was told that the baby would not make it my husband and I set off to Florida for vacation. This was a vacation with my parents, my brothers, my older brother's wife and two kids, my grandparents, and my uncle and his kids and grandchild. A lot of family, and a lot of opportunities for people to hint to Christopher and me that we should have kids soon. No one knew the deep ache in my heart. My little niece, probably only two years old at the time, at one point during the vacation came up to me and asked me when she would be getting a little baby cousin. My heart broke. I quietly left her standing there and walked into the bathroom and sobbed.

I was still not ready to accept this fate; however, and after a few more days I kept trying to tell myself that my baby was fine. I still didn't have any spotting or cramping... they must have made a mistake. I remember not going to Disney World while we were in Florida because I didn't want questions about why I wasn't going on any roller coasters. In my mind, the doctors were wrong. God was going to save my baby and everything was going to be okay. I remember not going into the hot tub at the pool because there was a sign warning against pregnant women going in the hot tub... again... denial. I remember standing in the shower and feeling my belly and standing there still feeling pregnant. I still *felt* pregnant. I remember still taking my prenatal vitamins and all the while I was in denial. I kept thinking that somehow, the doctors were wrong.

This denial went on for days, weeks even. I didn't have any outward signs of a miscarriage for almost five weeks. I think the Lord knew that I needed the time to process what was about to happen. My doctor gave me five weeks to miscarry naturally. If it did not occur within five weeks, I would have to have a D&C because there was risk for infection. Just a few days before the deadline I started spotting. Denial was no longer an option.

Next came a deep sadness and depression. I remember part of the miscarriage taking place in the bathtub... I had taken a bath hoping to alleviate some of the physical pain, and after I miscarried my second baby, I would not take a bath in that bathtub for months and months. I would step into the tub to even take a shower and I would just sob. All I could see in my mind was all the blood and I would relive those moments over and over. Depression began to hit hard. I desperately needed to talk to someone. I needed someone to understand. My husband would constantly ask me if there was anything he could do. I repeatedly told him no. There was nothing anyone could do. I remember crying when I would look at the trash can. When I miscarried the second time, a lot of blood and tissue ended up on paper towels in the trash. My precious baby, in the trash can. Words just simply are not enough to convey the depression and sadness in those moments. Even today, years later, I have a hard time writing about it. I remember a time where I didn't feel like eating or that life itself even mattered anymore. I remember feeling so hopeless and lost. I was confused and doubted God's plan for my life. So many questions plagued me. In the midst of this; however, God did not leave me.

Lamentations 3:22-26

"The steadfast love of the LORD never ceases;
his mercies never come to an end;
they are new every morning;
great is your faithfulness.
The LORD is my portion says my soul,
therefore I will hope in him.
The LORD is good to those who wait for him,
to the soul who seeks him.
It is good that one should wait quietly
for the salvation of the LORD."

I became very angry with God at one point. How could the all-powerful God let this happen to me? I was very angry. I remember thinking horrible things. I waited to have sex until I was married, so why is God punishing me? How is it that people have perfectly healthy children out of wedlock and I am stuck living in this nightmare of immense heartache? If God can do anything, why didn't he save my babies? When Hannah prayed, God gave her a child, so why couldn't I have one? These questions plagued my thoughts for a very long time after I lost my babies. The anger I felt was very real and very strong. I was miserable, and it felt like there was no way out. To make matters worse, I was surrounded by friends my age that were having healthy, beautiful babies.

That brings me to the next intense emotion that goes by the name of jealousy. That "green-eyed monster" has a way of consuming its victims. It goes hand in hand with its red cousin, anger. It seemed like every time I logged onto Facebook, another one of my friends was announcing they were pregnant, or had just welcomed a little one into the world. I was surrounded by people I should have been happy for, but all I could do was become angry and jealous. At one point I felt like punching pregnant women in the face. That sounds dramatic, and even a bit silly, but I was so angry and jealous, it was how I truly felt. Some of you have been there. I mentioned earlier about how God tells us in His Word that we are to "rejoice with those that rejoice." This was always an easy concept, until all of a sudden it wasn't. When you first hear that command it seems simple enough, but when you grow up and face life's trials, you quickly learn how truly hard it is. It is easy to be excited for someone when you are content and happy with where God has you in life, but when discontentment crowds in, jealousy is not far behind. I had to learn that Facebook was off-limits for a while, or I simply wasn't going to make it.

I felt like Job. Now, please hear me, I know my story is not nearly as difficult as Job's story, but it resonated with my soul. The basic concept of not understanding what was going on and questioning God…I totally understood that. Job questions God. Job did not understand why God was allowing him to lose everything, and yet Job did not sin and deny God. As time marched on, God showed me I needed to dig deep into His Word and look at the lives of those that suffered in Scripture. The life of Job has taught me many things. First of all, it is not wrong to question and even be angry. God's word says that Job did both of these, but that he did not sin. It is what you do with these emotions that can cause you to sin. Job questions God and is even angry, but in the end, He worships God anyways and remains faithful. Even when God seemed incredibly distant, Job remained faithful and clung to the truth of who God is.

Job 23:8-10

"Behold, I go forward, but he is not there,
and backward, but I do not perceive him;
on the left hand when he is working, I do not
behold him;
he turns to the right hand, but I do not see him.
But he knows the way that I take;
when he has tried me, I shall come out as gold."

God's ways are not our ways. His plans are not our plans. It is our job to simply trust and obey, even when we don't know the full story. It is so easy to read the account of Job, and pass over Job's faithfulness. We know the end of his story where God blesses Him immensely, and in reading God's Word we understand the reason for Job's suffering. Job didn't. He didn't know the ending of his story in the midst of his pain, and He didn't know this side of Heaven why God allowed his suffering. Job didn't know what God was doing or why, but he trusted God anyways. As difficult as it may be, we are called to do the same.

Ecclesiastes 11:5

"As you do not know the way the spirit comes to the bones in the womb of a woman with child, so you do not know the work of God who makes everything."

Take time right now and read Job chapters 38-42. It is a longer passage, but it talks of the greatness, majesty, and awesome power of the Almighty God. Please know and understand the truths found within these passages of scripture. The first truth is that God does not answer to us. God is the Creator of all things and He has the right to do what He wills. We are the created ones, and as such He does not owe us anything. This truth may seem a little harsh, but when coupled with the rest of these truths it is undeniably comforting. The next truth is that He is so much more powerful than your circumstances. Calling upon the title of Creator yet again, we see that God is powerful. He literally spoke the world into existence. Take a moment to contemplate the power that he possesses. Take some time to study the vastness of the universe and soak in just how powerful He really is. When you consider what he spoke into existence, you cannot deny that God is more powerful than your circumstances. Another truth is that He loves you beyond comprehension and without condition. God loves you more than you can ever know. He proved His love in the most extraordinary way when He sent His son to die a brutal and agonizing death on the cross for our sins. He sacrificed his Son, his only son, so that we could be redeemed. His love is beyond comprehension. Not only is it above and beyond what we can conceive, it is also without condition. It doesn't matter what you have done or been through. If you are a child of the King, you are loved unconditionally. When reflecting on those truths the only conclusion we can come to is that we can rest in His plan for our lives because we know beyond a shadow of a doubt that he loves us and desires the absolute best for us. The last truth is that He will use your circumstances for His glory. This means that no matter how much pain and suffering we go through, God can use it for good. He can use the circumstances that cause us pain to bring hope and life. It was through the pain of miscarriage that God brought me closer to Himself, and I was able to also reach out to others with hope from the Word of God.

Another emotion I faced, and probably one of the hardest I faced was actually a feeling of inadequacy. My husband and I both wanted children, and I was unable to have them. I felt like a failure as a wife. I remember apologizing over and over to my husband. I remember sobbing myself to sleep thinking, what if he leaves me because I cannot give him children. I praise God for my husband, and the compassion he showed me in those moments. Christopher would repeatedly reassure me that it was okay and that it was "our" problem of not being able to have kids, not just "my" problem. In my heart; however, I felt like I was solely to blame and it was all my fault. In my mind I knew that there was nothing I could do, but my heart was so broken. There is nothing worse than failing and not being able to do a single thing about it. I felt so powerless to do anything to make it right. I felt like I was letting my husband down, and our dreams of one day of having a family were shattered because of my inadequacy. I remember talking to my husband about adoption, but my heart ached for children of my own. There is nothing wrong with adoption, quite the opposite in fact. I even hope to adopt a child someday, but there was a part of me that wanted to carry that baby inside of me, to nurse that baby at my breast, and to look into his or her face and see bits and pieces of my husband and me formed into a precious baby.

I also remember talking to my husband about birth control. This one was hard. I did not want to keep getting pregnant and losing the baby. I simply could not do it anymore. I wanted to get my "tubes tied," but he was willing to possibly get a vasectomy. I kept thinking that if something happened to me where I died, and he wanted to remarry, it would be so unfair for me to have asked him to get a vasectomy. It was my problem, not his. He could have children, I could not. It was my fault, not his. I was the inadequate one. I distinctly remember one such conversation. We had gone for a walk at a nearby outdoor soccer complex by our house. It was a beautiful sunny day, but my heart was so incredibly dark and heavy. I told Christopher that we should think about me getting my tubes tied. I simply could not keep going through this over and over. I felt like it would have been different if I had already had a successful pregnancy. If I had a child and I knew that it was possible for my body to carry a baby to full term I could maybe endure at least one more try. Without that hope; however, I felt like this was it. This was the end of the road for us trying to have biological children. Christopher wisely told me not to jump to any conclusions just yet. We were going to at least wait for some test results to come back and see if they could figure out what was going on that was causing me to continue miscarrying my babies.

Psalm 34:18

"The LORD is near to the brokenhearted
and saves the crushed in spirit."

Part III

HEALING

THEY SAY THAT "TIME HEALS ALL wounds," but is that really true? I am now on the other side of my miscarriages, and this is what I can tell you: your wounds will heal but there will always be scars. There will be a part of you that will always grieve the loss you have suffered, but there is healing that takes place, and yes, time does help heal your wounds. To be honest, now even years later, I will still hesitate to take a bath, and I sob my eyes out when I hear of other women losing their babies, not only because I grieve for them, but it makes me relive losing mine. Time marches on; however, and it will get easier. You will never forget, but I promise you that you will one day feel hope again in your heart if you let God heal you.

I know that there are many different personalities out there, and not all women will benefit as dramatically as I did, but I do think that all women can benefit at least some in their healing process by sharing their story. Women were created to be compassionate and social beings. We love to talk and share. Women need other women, and going through miscarriage or any hard circumstance is when we need each other the most. I completely understand the desire to retreat into oneself, but trust me, in most cases it does more harm than good. Sharing what you are going through opens the door for other women to show you the love of Christ in a very tangible way. God uses other women in our lives to show us compassion, and to walk with us through the storms of life.

Please hear me when I say you need to share your story with Godly women. These women are those that will keep your story in confidence if that is what you request, and these are women that are mature in Christ. Choose someone in your life that will not judge your emotions, and if possible they have experienced the loss of a child as well. You do not need to share with someone who will judge you for being angry with God, or someone that will blab your heartache to others. You need someone that will be non-judgmental while you vent your feelings, and will pray with you that God comes in and heals your heart. For those of you out there that do not have anyone that fits these qualifications, find someone. Look within the local church for women who are mature believers. God's Word says you will know them by their fruit. Pray that God brings such women into your life to walk with you through this journey.

Sharing your story can be done in many different ways. If you are a more private person, sharing one-on-one can be most effective. If you are a little more outgoing you can blog or use social media to share your story. This is a way for others to see what you have gone through and it opens the door for other women who have had miscarriages to help you. If we don't share our stories, others won't know who to turn to for help.

When I was in high school, I had a small group leader in our church youth group that had gone through infertility and miscarriages. One night in youth groups she shared her struggles. She didn't get into details, and it wasn't a long conversation, but it stuck with me. She had briefly talked about what she had gone through to the girls in our group and then talked about the sovereignty and grace of God. Fast forward to over ten years later, and I am now going through my miscarriages. The Holy Spirit brings my previous youth leader's name to mind, and I immediately know what I have to do. I had been silent for so long about what was going on, and it was time for me to seek help from someone I knew had experienced a very similar hardship in her past. This youth leader was used by God to help heal my soul and provide compassion, prayer, and encouragement. Can you imagine if she hadn't shared her story? I would have had a much harder road if she had not followed the prompting of God to share her story ten years earlier to a group of high school girls.

2 Corinthians 1:3-4

> "Blessed be the God and Father of our
> Lord Jesus Christ, the Father of mercies
> and God of all comfort, who comforts
> us in all our affliction, so that we may
> be able to comfort those who are in any
> affliction, with the comfort with which
> we ourselves are comforted by God."

This is why I want to share my story. This is why we all should share our story. We need each other. We need to stop pretending we have it all together and our lives are perfect, because, let's face it, no one is falling for it. We all go through tough times, and it's about time that we allow vulnerability and transparency to enter into our lives. I am in no way saying you need to announce your struggles to the world, but be willing to share your story. Listen to the Holy Spirit's prompting in your heart so that you may allow God to use others to comfort you as well as give you opportunities to comfort those around you.

My sharing came in waves. I first shared my story with my previous youth leader in the midst of my deepest pain. This was for the sake of my own healing. After I shared my story with her I was then able to share my story with many of my colleagues and even in front of many women at my church for a women's event. I will tell you that God has opened so many doors for me to speak the truth of God's love and compassion into the lives of so many women. I have had women that I have talked to in person, and others that have reached out to me via social media to ask me questions and seek comfort after losing a child. It is only because I listened to God's leading to share my story that I have been used by God to be able to help so many women. Isn't that how it should be? God created the Church so that we could not only worship together, but so that we could edify and speak truth into our fellow believers' lives.

So what is the truth? What truth in God's word helps heal wounds from having a miscarriage? Remember Hannah whom I alluded to earlier? Let's take a quick look at her story in the first chapter of 1 Samuel.

Hannah was married to a man named Elkanah. Elkanah also happened to have a second wife, which was not uncommon during Old Testament times. His second wife went by the name Peninnah, and the Scriptures say that she had many sons and daughters with Elkanah. Meanwhile, Hannah was barren. Take a step back and think about this for a moment. Imagine being married to this man, and not only do you have to share him with his other wife, but imagine his other wife having a ton of children, and you are unable to have any. Talk about jealousy and heartache.

The passage reads that Hannah at one point was so upset and depressed about her situation that she was weeping and wouldn't even eat. Her husband, bless his heart, asks her why she is so upset. He asks her why he isn't enough. He literally asks her the question, "Do I not mean more to you than ten sons?" What Elkanah does not understand is that many women truly desire in their hearts to be a mother. It wasn't that she didn't love her husband or appreciate him, but having a husband is not the same as having children. God wired most women with a nurturing spirit and a desire to have kids, and that desire runs deep. Think of all the money a couple will spend on infertility doctors and IVF. Women desire to carry a baby, their baby, in their womb.

How does Hanna respond in her time of distress though? She prays. She doesn't just ask God "willy-nilly" for a baby. She cries out to her God in such a way that a priest nearby thinks she is drunk. In Hannah's story, God grants her the desire of her heart and a short time later she welcomes her son into the world. God is more powerful than any of our circumstances.

Good for her, you may be thinking, but what about me. Does that mean that if I pray fervently for a child, or pray that I won't have any more miscarriages that God will grant me my request? The answer: maybe. God may have that in store for you, or He may have a different plan for your life. You see, the truth is that we live in a fallen world, and things don't always go the way we plan, BUT God does promise to walk with you every step of the way if you just let Him. God will bring about good for His glory even in the midst of hardship.

Many of you, like me, may have struggled with that all too well known verse, Romans 8:28. This verse says "And we know that for those who love God all things work together for good, for those who were called according to His purpose." I cannot tell you how much I struggled with this verse. I loved (and still do love) God. After I miscarried the second time all I could think was, *I am a faithful wife, I serve in our local church, I do my devotions and have a good prayer life…why on earth would God allow this to happen to me?* You see, like many others I was under the impression that if I did what I was supposed to do then God would do what I thought He was supposed to do. He would protect me from harm, He would work out things for the good in my life… and I was having a really hard time seeing the good! Thankfully, God did not leave me in this place of deep questioning and doubt. He ordained a talk for me with a dear friend of mine. She pointed out to me the following verse. Romans 8:29 says "For those whom He foreknew He also predestined to be conformed to the image of His Son, in order that He might be the first-born among many brothers." Now we are not going to get into God's foreknowledge or the theology of pre-destination. Those are topics for another day, but look at the next phrase, "…to be conformed to the image of His Son…" That's the bullseye. This verse goes hand in hand with the one before it, so it cannot be ignored. God uses the situations in our life to transform us. He uses trials to make us more like His Son, Jesus Christ.

You see, no matter what happens, good or bad, God will use it for the good. When the effects of sin and evil in this world cause something terrible to happen in our lives, God will use it for His glory. It doesn't mean we won't have incredibly difficult times, because we all know that we will; it means that through those times God will shape and mold our hearts to become more like Christ. Isn't that the ultimate reason we are on this Earth? To share the Gospel with others and to become more like Christ. It is not an easy truth to swallow at times, but it is a truth nonetheless. It is a truth that promises beauty from ashes. It promises that good will always win in the end. It promises that God is so much bigger than the problems we face.

I praise God every day that my story has evolved into an ending similar to Hannah's. After years of waiting and miscarriages, God has blessed us with a beautiful baby boy. His name is Sawyer Jamison, but although he is my biological son, he does not belong to me. You see, my husband and I have learned through all of this that everything we have, everything we are, every blessing we receive, is of God. Sawyer is a gift from God, and we are to be good and Godly stewards of this precious little boy He has given us. I have some dear friends that gave me a plaque to hang in his room that has more of Hannah's story written on it. It reads:

> "For this child I prayed, and the LORD has granted me my petition that I made to him. Therefore I have lent him to the LORD. As long as he lives, he is lent to the LORD." I Samuel 1:27-28

Sawyer is not ours, He is the Lord's. Should the Lord choose to take him as he took his other two siblings, I must accept that. Through this God has shown me that I must love Him above all else. I must be as Abraham was when he was willing to sacrifice his son to prove that he loved God above all else. Following Christ is not easy. It is not always fun. It is not always fair by human standards. It can be extremely hard. It can be very demanding. It can be filled with sorrow.

But I am convinced that it is all worth it. I will one day see my precious babies that I never held on this earth, and when I meet Jesus someday, when I stand face to face with my Savior in glory, I want to hear "well done, my good and faithful servant." In the meantime, I will praise God and allow Him to, no matter what happens or doesn't happen in my life, change me into the image of His Son, Jesus Christ. Will you?

Revelation 21:4

> "He will wipe away every tear from their eyes, and death shall be no more, neither shall there be mourning, nor crying, nor pain anymore, for the former things have passed away."

Another way that can help the healing process is to write a letter to the child(ren) that you lost. This can be a way to acknowledge the pain and also work though it in a way that is more tangible. It is not an easy process, and it will inevitably cause tears to fall, but it also gives an opportunity for healing. It allows you to say good-bye for now to the precious little one that was gone far too soon. I will share with you my letter. I wrote this to my two precious babies.

My dearest little ones,

Mommy loves you beyond words, and I miss you both terribly. I miss thinking of all the fun things we were going to do once you got here. My arms ache to hold you and my ears long to hear your giggles. My eyes yearn for the day when I can look into your sweet eyes and see your arms reach out for me. I wish your daddy and I could have met you, but even though we never laid eyes on you, we love you so very much. We want you to know that you are so precious to us, and we cannot wait to meet you someday. We know that you are in the strong and loving arms of our Savior, and that gives us great comfort to know you are safe and protected. We rejoice that you never knew the harshness that this world can bring, that you never had to know fear or pain. I often wonder what you would have been like. What would your favorite color have been? Would you have loved ice cream and chocolate as much as I do? Would you be an incessant talker like me or have a quiet strength like your daddy?

What would you have been when you grew up? I love you, my precious babies, and I grieve the fact that these questions will go unanswered, but I am so thankful that this is not the end. We will meet you someday, and I cannot wait to finally hold you in my arms. Until then, know you are so incredibly loved.

Until our "someday" finally comes,
Mommy

I told you. Tears will come. There is no real healing without them. This is just another way that may help you to gain some closure and healing. Ultimately, it is God who does the healing, but he has given us different tools and also different people in our lives to help us along this painful journey. My prayer for you is that you are able to find ways that help you to overcome the pain and allow God to heal your heart. Like I have said, your heart will heal, but there will always be scars. The scars; however, are reminders of God's incredible love and faithfulness even in the midst of our darkest days.

PART IV

WHERE MY JOURNEY LED ME

IF I HAD TO SUM UP MY MISCARRIAGES IN one word, it's trust. It is summed up in the lack of it, and then its beautiful strengthening. For those of us who have grown up living in the church, we are very familiar with the verse in Proverbs that says, "Trust in the Lord with all your heart." I learned this verse when I was probably only four years old. It's been hammered into my brain from such a young age, and I was fully convinced of its meaning; up until I reached the darkness of losing my two children that is. Trusting God is not something that comes easily, at least not to me. My brain was well aware that even in the darkest of moments that God was still in control, and that I was commanded to trust Him. My heart; however, needed some convincing. As I have stated before, I am very independent and I like "all of my ducks in a row." This type of personality finds it extremely hard to let go and allow God to sit in the driver's seat. When we lost our precious little babies I felt like my world was crashing down around me. I felt helpless. I HATE feeling helpless, that there is absolutely nothing I can do. I like to fix things, come up with creative solutions to problems, and take charge when something needs to be done. But when you experience a miscarriage, you quickly realize that nothing can be done. There was no way for me to fix the situation, to creatively solve the problem… so I spiraled.

The depression was very real and very deep, and my lack of trust in God in those moments was what kept me in that depression for far too long. I had to learn that trusting God meant even when I didn't understand, when I saw no way out, and when my pain was so unbearable that I couldn't stand it, I still had to let Him be in control and trust His plan. Especially then. It was through opening up to others in my life that I began to stop blaming and hating God, and I learned what it meant to TRULY trust in Him. I learned how to trust not just when things were going well, but even more so when the sky was falling. Trust is a daily choice. It is a moment by moment choice.

If you have ever read the account of the Israelites in the desert in the Old Testament, you know that you must choose to trust every single day. When I read their story, I often think that they were so dumb. They literally had pillars of fire and clouds to guide them, they walked on dry land across a sea, and they were brought out of slavery and bondage through incredible miracles. God provided manna and water for them. He gave them laws and instructions to live by... and yet their story is riddled with times of severe doubt and mistrust toward God. I tend to look at that and think that I could never act like they did, that surely I would not be as dense as the Israelites, but news flash: I was. I was exactly like them. My story is full of cases where God has intervened and provided for my needs. He provided jobs for me, the finances I needed for college, He provided me with an incredible and loving husband and family... and even more amazing is He provided me with the miracle of salvation, and yet when my life became impossibly difficult, I chose to blame Him.

It seems so ignorant and stupid when I read back those words to myself. I had so many reasons to trust, but I chose not to. Why? Why did I choose to blame God? Why did I choose anger over trust? I have no answer for you other than that I am still at war with my flesh. As Paul writes in the New Testament, we are at war with our sinful nature. Even if you are a child of God, you will still sin, you will still choose the wrong thing at times. This was one of those times for me. I praise God every day that He stepped in and didn't leave me there. He didn't hear my anger and say, "Well, since you seem to be mad at me, I'm done, I'm out." No… my incredible, loving, merciful God stepped in and in so many different places in scripture said, "I understand your hurt. I too lost a Son. I lost my Son willingly for a wicked and sinful people. I know you are angry, but I am here. I am not going anywhere. Nothing can separate us. You are my child, and you are loved."

God used this time in my life to teach me what it means to fully, completely, and without any reservation or hesitation, trust in Him. His grace fills my story, and it has led me to some incredible things in my life.

God saw fit to bless me with a third pregnancy after I lost my two babies. Even in this I struggled with trust. Every day was a struggle to fight the anxiety and fear of having to walk the path of extreme loss yet again. Even though God had seen me through the first two losses, and allowed me to become pregnant again, there were no guarantees. I remember being absolutely terrified to go to the bathroom for my entire pregnancy. I was always afraid that when I was done that I would see that red stain of blood on the toilet paper. I had to battle with anxiety attacks and sleepless nights, trying to trust that no matter what, God was still in control and demanded my complete trust.

When I was past my first trimester, I finally felt ready to tell some people that I was pregnant. I cautiously told some family members, and then shared with many people at church that I was expecting a little one. At the time of my third pregnancy I was teaching fifth grade at a Christian school, and I also shared with the faculty my story of loss and the fact that I was pregnant. I shared how the doctors had figured out that the issue was low progesterone, and I was confident that this was finally going to be my miracle baby. I even shared with my students that I was pregnant. I shared my exciting news with all of the different people in my life over the course of a week.

Friday night came, and so did some deep anxiety. I woke up very late Friday night, or rather very early Saturday morning, and the bed was very wet. Immediately I thought I was leaking amniotic fluid. My heart was so incredibly anxious in that moment. The level of fear and stress is so hard to describe, and unless you have walked through something similar, it is hard to understand. At this point I had totally abandoned the thought of trusting God with this baby. I tried to once again sit in the driver's seat and control the situation instead of trusting. I was a mess. My husband awoke to find me on the couch, silently staring at seemingly nothing while tears streamed down my face. I just looked at him with empty eyes. I had to wait for a few hours until my OBGYN office opened and I was able to schedule an emergency ultrasound. I truly cannot describe those hours of waiting to you. Some of you may know from experience, but it is an outer body type experience of disbelief and pain. As we drove to get the ultrasound my tears had stopped, and were replaced by indifference and denial. It was easier to pretend that I didn't care, but my heart was shattered. I had been down this road before. I didn't think I could make it again.

My husband and I went into the back room to get the ultrasound. My mind and heart were racing as we sat there quietly awaiting what the technician would say. Finally, she said, "everything looks good, there is plenty of amniotic fluid, and the baby is moving around. Looks like you have a future dancer in there!" I couldn't believe my ears. Everything was fine? You mean that the other shoe that I have been so sure was going to drop is not even there? In that moment God whispered into my heart, "I told you, I've got this. I have you, Amy. Why do you fight Me? Why do you refuse to trust Me?" I was utterly relieved and ashamed all at the same time. I was so thankful that my baby was safe and sound, but I could not believe my level of distrust. I was just like those Israelites. Don't get me wrong, this was definitely a situation that called for some concern, but my level of complete distrust should not have been what it was. So believe me when I say that I am still a work in progress.

I do not have it all figured out, and I still to this day struggle with trusting God completely, but in the midst of all of these trials and circumstances God has grown me tremendously in this area.

My miscarriage journey has also led me to be very involved with sanctity of life organizations. When I lost my babies, I knew that they were human beings, they were a life, a precious life made in the image of God. That is why losing them had been so incredibly hard. God used my loss to burden my heart for unborn babies that are voluntarily killed, and for the mothers of these babies. Many of these women feel as if they have no choice, and they come from extremely difficult situations. God opened my eyes to the need for action. God led me to work with an amazing organization that works with moms to help them with the adoption process, or to support them if they choose to keep their baby. They don't just help the mom until that baby is born, but continue to support the mom as she raises her child. The goal of this ministry is to share the love and Gospel of Jesus with these women and children, and I thank God that He used my story of pain and loss to lead me to work with this organization. That is what God does. He takes the ugly, broken things of this world, and uses them for His honor and glory.

God has also used my loss to lead me to a place of deep gratefulness. I am so thankful for my baby boy. I have my days where things can be challenging, but then God reminds me about what a miracle he is, and my heart is overwhelmed with gratitude. Not only am I grateful for my son, but I am thankful for God's grace. This journey has led me to a place where I have experienced the grace of God in such real and powerful ways. He carried me when I couldn't go on. He loved me through the darkness. He never once gave up on me, even in my most stubborn moments of mistrust. God's grace is sufficient, and I am so thankful that God turned my heartache into blessing. Even if I was not blessed with a child to hold, or even if God allowed my son Sawyer to be taken from me, He is still good. He is still God. He is still in control, and I will choose to trust Him.

PART V

THE STORIES
OF OTHERS

WHILE IN THE PROCESS OF WRITING THIS book, I thought it may be helpful for you as the reader to hear from other women as well. I asked three of my dear friends to write out their stories of struggle and hope, in order that you may find comfort in their words as well. These words were written by their own hand and used with their full permission in the hopes of yet again touching your heart and helping you heal.

The first woman to share her story is Connie Okupski. I have known Connie since I was about nine years old. Our friendship got off to a rocky start in the fourth grade, but as God would intervene we ended up at the same church and eventually became very good friends. She is now the faithful wife of a youth pastor and a loving mother to their daughter Aliya. They currently serve at a church in Pennsylvania.

This is Connie's story:

From the very start of our marriage, my husband and I were excited to have a family. While others talked about their "five year plan" to work and save for a while before having kids, I think we started talking about kids before we returned from our honeymoon. The big unknown of "having kids" was such an exciting thing to me- would we have a boy or girl first? What would we name our baby?

We managed to wait about a year and a half before we both felt ready to go ahead and try to get pregnant. We ended up getting pregnant the very first month (!) and the pregnancy flew by, with both of us working full time and finishing our master's degrees before baby Marshall arrived. The pregnancy was smooth and easy, and our daughter Aliya Joy was born in October 2016. She was an overall happy and healthy baby, for which we were so thankful. Before Aliya was a year old, my husband wanted to try for another! I laughed him off, told him I had JUST had a baby, and said I would let him know when I was ready. When Aliya was about a year and a half, we started trying again.

This time it took three months to become pregnant. When we found out we were pregnant again, we were overjoyed and quickly told our family and closest friends. We put a "Best Big Sister" shirt on Aliya and took pictures. We were in the process of moving a couple states away during this process, so I called my OB/GYN office and slyly asked if I could have an early doctor's appointment to "make sure the baby was ok" before we moved. This was my way of trying to hear the baby's heartbeat sooner than we would normally be scheduled to! That request ended up being God's way of protecting us. The doctor consented to an early ultrasound and sent me for bloodwork to see when the baby would be big enough to view via ultrasound. However, it soon became clear that my HCG (the pregnancy hormone) was low and was not doubling every day as it should.

The doctor's office told me that miscarriage was likely. However, I didn't quite believe them, as my sister-in-law had gone through something similar and had still ended up having a healthy baby. After a few ultrasounds to check and thinking maybe we just weren't as far along as we thought, it was determined that our baby was indeed not growing. There was no heartbeat visible on the ultrasound, and since babies grow so rapidly in the beginning, it was clear that the pregnancy was not thriving. Being warned I would miscarry, I chose to let things proceed naturally. I started spotting that night, and miscarried the next day. We were 8 weeks along, although the baby hadn't grown past 5 weeks.

I think that no matter how far along you are, miscarriage is always hard. However, during this miscarriage, I felt very protected and cushioned by God. We had many doctor appointments to process that we could possibly miscarry, and at our last appointment, found out that we would certainly miscarry. Therefore, when the actual miscarriage happened, I felt prepared for the event, so it wasn't too traumatic. I bled a great deal, and then went on with our plans to go to a church cookout. I wasn't being on-the-go in an unhealthy way, but felt that I did want to stay busy and be around people during this time, even if they didn't know what we were going through.

My biggest question for the doctor was when we could try again. I am an optimistic and upbeat person by nature, so I was ready to bounce back and provide our Aliya Joy with a sibling! Our daughter was by that time almost two, and as sweet and nurturing as they come. She started to enjoy playing with baby dolls, and would point with wonder at every baby she saw in the grocery store. By this time, I was eager for her to become a big sister. I thought I was going to be pregnant in April, so to be in August and to have an empty womb was not what I had expected. My doctor said we could try again as soon as my period returned, so that's what we did!

I was relieved to see my period return in a month. I carefully tracked everything in my fertility app, to figure out my fertile window. We became pregnant again right away, much to our joy and relief! This pregnancy was different from the start. My belly seemed to start growing immediately. I felt more tired and lost my appetite. I was cautiously optimistic. Our due date was June 20, 2019. We started to make plans accordingly. At the 12 week mark, we considered ourselves in the clear. We had heard the heartbeat early on, and had even gotten to see our squirming baby in an ultrasound at 10 weeks. I strongly suspected it was a boy based on how much different I felt from when I was pregnant with Aliya. At 12 ½ weeks, we shared with our youth group (my husband is a youth pastor) that we were expecting. People were starting to guess about my growing belly anyway!

The next day, I went to bed tired and with a stomach ache. My mind filled with dread as soon as I realized that my stomach ache was not gas, but actually contractions. I labored through the late night, and woke up at 1:30 in the morning with the mattress beneath me soaked in the blood. I went into the bathroom and passed a lot of blood. I was dry heaving and breaking out in a cold sweat. I'm sure I passed the baby during this time, but by the grace of God, I didn't see the baby in all the blood. I'm sure that would be an image that would never leave my mind.

Waking up the next day and realizing the "baby lump" that I felt each morning was completely gone was probably the worst feeling I have ever experienced. I think that despite the traumatic night, there had been a tiny sliver of hope that it was just some strange bleeding and that there was still a healthy baby in my womb. Our primary feeling in all of this was shock. We were more than 12 weeks, almost to the second trimester. My belly had been big. The pregnancy seemed to be thriving. How could we have lost another baby? The next day was filled with tears, as we had an ultrasound confirming no baby was in my uterus. We were heartbroken.

In all this, God felt absent. I felt unsure of what to pray for, and just felt numb and shocked. I really did not want a D&C procedure, but was afraid that due to being farther along and due to God seeming to want to test me, that I would end up needing one. Thankfully, 3 days later, I had more contractions, and my body passed more tissue. I didn't end up needing a D&C, for which I was thankful. I came around slowly to God. I had always had a strong faith and didn't understand why people quickly questioned God in hard times. This was a true test of my faith, though. The Holy Spirit reminded me that I could not sing praises one day when I was pregnant and simply stop praising the next day because my circumstances had changed. I had to remember in the darkness what I had learned in the light. I struggled with God not feeling near, but it was also Christmastime. I came to realize that Christmastime is the ultimate time of God coming near to us, by sending his son Jesus to earth to save us from our sins. How could I accuse God of being far away? I accepted the miscarriage as a sad part of our story and grew eager to try again.

I will say that the aftermath of the second miscarriage almost seemed harder than the miscarriage itself. If I could coin a term for what I experienced, it would be medical re-traumatization. Now, some doctor's offices are fantastic. In our situation, this was not the case. Throughout the time of doing blood work and ultrasounds after the miscarriage to make sure all the pregnancy tissue passed and the pregnancy hormone worked its way out of my system, I experienced much frustration. I would often have to call and leave messages with the doctor's office, and wait for a call back from someone completely different. I would have to repeat my story over and over. I would frustrate medical assistants or receptionists or receptionists with questions, and they would have to go ask the doctor, and someone else would call me hours later. At times I would call asking for the next step of doctor's orders, and wouldn't get a call back all day, only to get a call back at the end of the day asking if I could rush in for blood work that night. I try to not be the kind of person who complains about bad customer service or when things are poorly run;

however, when I was approaching this particular office with an open, sensitive, hurting heart, all the confusion and having so much difficulty reaching someone who knew me and my story was a huge stressor.

I ended up doing the blood work that my OB/GYN had offered to see if there could be a reason why I was miscarrying. This tested for things like thyroid issues and blood clotting disorders. The tests, as I expected, came back clear. Many women who had also had miscarriages mentioned progesterone to me, so I began to wonder if low progesterone (which is necessary to sustain a pregnancy in the first trimester until the placenta takes over supporting the pregnancy) could be at play and could have caused our second miscarriage.

When I first brought up the idea of testing for low progesterone, the staff on the phone (I'm unsure if she was a medical assistant or a nurse) was skeptical, as if she wanted to discourage me from the testing. When I brought up a few symptoms I was having, such as spotting mid-cycle, she cynically asked if it could be from having sex. Her insensitivity and condescension was shocking to me. I have always tried to advocate for my own health and felt like the medical staff were just wanting me to sit down and listen. I felt throughout this process that the medical community only viewed things from a macro level ("One in three pregnancies end in miscarriage"), so they weren't willing to see things from a micro level ("What if there could be something causing THIS particular miscarriage?"). I know the statistics and understand that miscarriage is common. I had researched reliable sources on miscarriage. However, I feel like a patient's gut feelings should not be dismissed for statistics and general studies. I truly thought it through and realized I was not trying to control the uncontrollable (many miscarriages are random and totally unpreventable). I had a gut feeling that something was off, and I felt like no one at the doctor's office believed me. I was told that miscarriage often isn't looked into until after three pregnancy losses. However, after already going through the intense emotion of losing two very loved and desired pregnancies, I wanted to prevent a third loss if at all possible.

Thankfully, my OB was kind and gracious during this time, and said we could do a biopsy at the end of my next cycle to see if my progesterone levels were where they should be. That's where we are at now. I wish I could end my story saying that all is well, and we are happily pregnant again, but we aren't quite there yet. At this point, it's a waiting game. It's been 2 cycles since the last miscarriage, and all that can go through my mind is "we can have an October baby." "Okay, maybe a November baby." Now, it looks like December may be the earliest. I look at other families and see gaps of three, four, or even more years, and remind myself that it's okay that our daughter will be more than 3 when she has her first sibling. However, it can be so hard to be patient. I find myself wishing pregnancy weren't a long nine months long. I'm happy for those on Facebook I see with new babies, but it doesn't come without a sad wistfulness as well. Life with a newborn seems like ages ago, and it feels like it will be forever until we'll be there again. I've changed a little too, and have become a little wiser and probably a little more somber at times too. I worry for those announcing their pregnancies very early on. Pregnancy used to be a simple and easy thing to me, but no more.

In all this though, I'm trying to find the positive. Some find that momentos of their lost little ones are helpful, but for me, that would only be a sad, sad reminder. It's been most helpful for me to move on and find the positive. We are planning a vacation for our family this year and doing our best to relish life as a family of 3. I went on a sushi date with my husband (something I could not enjoy if I were pregnant!). I eat cookie dough. I go in the hot tub at the gym. I'm more active and eating better to take better care of myself. I've found several songs that speak to my soul when I'm tempted to pity myself. I try to soak in Aliya's two-year-old antics as much as I can, and remember that someday I will look back at the timeline of our family and be so thankful that I had several years just with her. I do wish I were pregnant, but since I'm not, I will live for things other than a pregnancy. I will hope and pray for a child, but I will not allow longing for a new baby to consume me and steal the joy that I have in my husband and my little girl.

Kymber Klinger is a dear friend of mine. God allowed the two of us to work together teaching at a Christian school, and God graciously allowed me to walk with Kymber through her experience. It is because I had the courage to speak out about my miscarriages that I was able to help in some small way as Kymber went through her miscarriage journey. I remember when she and I would talk about our struggles with pregnancy. She would talk about how she and her husband had been trying for so long to get pregnant, and I would talk about the loss of my babies. We would joke together about wanting to sometimes punch pregnant women in the face (it was just the anger and frustration talking… we would never actually do something like that). We would talk about how it was so hard to see all of our friends getting pregnant and feeling happy for them, and yet immensely jealous at that same time.

I specifically remember when Kymber walked into my classroom and started sobbing. It was Grandparents Day at school and the kids and their grandparents would be arriving shortly. She walked into my room and simply said, "this is worse, so much worse." Kymber then went on to explain that they had finally gotten pregnant, only to then lose the baby. My heart was so broken for her. She was walking the path that I had just come out of, and I knew her pain was so incredibly deep and real. We have been through a lot together, and she is one of the strongest women I know.

This is Kymber's Story:

I admit I am a little bit of a control freak. If something goes unexpectedly or not the way I think it should, I tend to get a little anxious. I always say that I was meant to be a teacher because I am in control of how my room is run, which is something that comforts that control freak in me. So when something does go wrong or something is unjust, bad, unexpected, or in any way different than what I wanted, I knew I had two choices. Do I get angry, cry out in anger, say this isn't fair, throw in the towel…or thank God, turn to Him and try to find out what He is teaching me.

Trusting God and knowing He has a better plan, or that He knows what's best and is ultimately the one in control is extremely hard sometimes. My initial reaction, and I am sure some of yours as well, is to react negatively…but that is not what the answer should be. I know that when I get angry, these thoughts and words come out of my mouth… "God why me? I can't handle this! Please no…" But over the past 10+ years I've had to learn that getting and staying angry just makes it all worse. It is not what God wants. He wants to teach me something and bring me closer to Him, even if that means it happens through trials, tribulations, questions, and anger.

In February 2008, my father passed away quickly and extremely unexpectedly. He wasn't sick, didn't have any chronic illnesses and was, as far as he knew, "healthy." One Saturday, everything started off normal as he and I joked together and sat talking just before he wished my mom and I a good day at work. When I got home my life changed forever. I found him dead, and as a 20 year old young girl, it turned my life upside down. Instantly, I was hurting and I was angry. "God why? I am a good girl, I go to church. I am a Christian, I have good friends. I don't drink, I don't smoke"…so on and so on…

I struggled for a few years. I started not caring. I clung to the anger and it ate me up inside knowing that I was turning from the only One who could truly give me comfort.

Psalm 13: 1-4

"How long, O Lord? Will you forget me forever?
How long will you hide your face from me?
² How long must I take counsel in my soul
and have sorrow in my heart all the day?
How long shall my enemy be exalted over me?
³ Consider and answer me, O Lord my God;
light up my eyes, lest I sleep the sleep of death,
⁴ lest my enemy say, "I have prevailed over him,"

lest my foes rejoice because I am shaken.

I finally pulled myself together. It wasn't easy, but I decided my anger wasn't going to control me.

All was good until my husband and I tried to start our own family. Well, even though the control freak inside of me was trying all the tricks and tips of the trade, nothing worked. After a full year and half we decided to go to Buffalo IVF in June 2016 for a little extra assistance. They are not cheap but we longed for a family of our own. After some initial tests, fertility drugs and extremely close monitoring we got pregnant in September. Yes! Awesome! We were thrilled as you can imagine. We were busting at the seams to tell people, but knowing we couldn't at such an early time. In November, that all changed. A routine ultrasound turned into the baby we longed for, no longer growing or thriving. It was a punch to the heart and a complete shock for my husband and myself. We'd been trying so hard only to have our dream stopped once more.

I felt myself going to my anger for comfort. Back to the questions for God, the "why me's" and the "what did I do wrong." I knew that would be a very easy slope to slip back down, but I also knew it would get me nowhere. Instead of growing apart because of this set back, my husband and I grieved together and leaned on one another for support. We found joy in thinking my dad was cradling our baby and taking care of him/her until we were able to be with our baby ourselves.

So January 2017 comes and we get pregnant again. Wow! No way! Thank you Lord for such a quick blessing! February, the day before my dad's anniversary, we lost another baby. Now remember last school year there were 5 pregnant mamas around me. As undeniably happy and excited I was for them, it only made it harder on me. I struggled, I cried, and I grieved, but again didn't let the anger control me. My new question became, God what are you teaching me through this? I am trusting that You know what is best.

Psalms 13:5-6

"⁵ But I have trusted in your steadfast love;
my heart shall rejoice in your salvation.
⁶ I will sing to the LORD,
because he has dealt bountifully with me."

After extensive and expensive testing, my amazing doctor was able to pinpoint a potential problem that was preventing my babies from growing. I have an extremely rare genetic blood disorder that prevents my body from easily breaking down clots. Now a light clicks for me going "oh my goodness, could this tie back to potentially why my dad died?" With it being genetic there is a high chance that my father had a clot that we didn't know of and it ultimately became a bigger problem. My paternal grandfather also died suddenly around the same age as my father. My brother recently had surgery and dealt with a blood clot that was unexpected and not easily treatable. Did God use my infertility as a way to help keep my family safe? Now my uncle, brothers and nieces/nephews are all getting a blood test to check PAI – 1protien mutation. This blood disorder normally wouldn't show up in a routine blood test, so it is only by God that we now know and can express it to our doctors before we have any sort of surgery. So for me, this meant for the duration of any pregnancies I would need to take a shot every day. Shockingly I got pregnant again (without fertility meds) and began my new medicine regimen. 200 plus shots later I finally got to hold my gift from God, my miracle, my baby girl.

I could've let anger seep in and turn my two losses into a deep depression. I could've given up and said I just can't do this anymore, but instead I realized God is in control of it all. There was and is a reason I went through all of what I did. I trusted He was in control and sought out an amazing woman, who had gone through miscarriages like me, for comfort. In Ezekiel, God reminds us he is always taking care of His flock, even when the clouds and darkness seem to loom over our head.

Ezekiel 34:12

"12 As a shepherd seeks out his flock when he is among his sheep that have been scattered, so will I seek out my sheep, and I will rescue them from all places where they have been scattered on a day of clouds and thick darkness."

Now I can use my circumstances for good. My tragedy with my dad has allowed me to come alongside others and comfort them in situations like this. Recently, I learned of my very good friends who are also going through fertility issues. I can now give them advice and grieve alongside them while comforting them as well. Don't let your anger get in the way of God teaching you and using your hardships for His glory.

Stephanie and I went to college together in Pennsylvania. As with a lot of people, my college years were some of the greatest years of my young life. Stephanie and I have some amazing memories of late night study sessions, road trips to Lancaster, shopping, and just hanging out together in the dorms. We became good friends our sophomore year, and we have stayed in touch ever since. She has been through so much since those 'good old days,' but she remains faithful and hopeful in the midst of such heartache. She is incredibly strong and I am honored to know her as a dear friend. I pray her courageous story helps encourage you in your own journey.

This is Stephanie's Story:

Unexplained recurrent miscarriages. Those are not the words I ever expected to hear from my doctor. How could I have this diagnosis? I grew up dreaming of the day I would meet that perfect somebody. We would get married and have so many babies (SIX to be exact!) …I loved children so how could one expect any less of my dreams? When I finally found that perfect someone and we decided we were ready to start a family, little did I know my world would be turned upside down trying to create that dream of mine. I went off of birth control in January 2016 and assumed it might take a couple of months, but I never doubted it would happen. Soon a couple months turned into over a year and still nothing. I sought out the advice of my OBGYN where I received the hard diagnosis of PCOS…anyone with PCOS knows how rough it is living with all those symptoms! My doctor put me on metformin in February 2017 and once I had worked up to the full dosage, I noticed it was helping my irregular period become a little more predictable. Then in June of that year I finally saw those two beautiful pink lines I had been hoping to see for so long! I was over the moon. I started buying little outfits and daydreaming about what that little one inside me would become someday. However, just a few short weeks later I started bleeding. I was, of course, panicked, but kept telling myself everything must be okay. We were not so lucky. We had lost our first baby and I was devastated.

Once my period had finally come back a couple months later, I found myself faced with those two pink lines again, on my birthday nonetheless. I still could not help but be overjoyed because I told myself it was fairly common to miscarry your first so this time would be different. Then on Thanksgiving Day....just a few short days after getting a positive test, I started bleeding again. Why was this happening?

This is where my faith started wavering a bit. Why was God allowing this to happen a second time? Wasn't taking my first baby from me enough? I was angry, confused, and hurting. What do we do now, I thought to myself. I immediately scheduled an appointment with my doctor and discussed where to go from there. She said I wouldn't be diagnosed with recurrent miscarriages with "only two losses". She said we would keep trying and if I lost another one then we could test the tissue to see if there was some abnormality. I walked out of there feeling so lost and not a lot of answers on why I was losing my babies.

After promising me she was going to help get me pregnant, my doctor retired and the whole practice closed down so I had to search for a new doctor. While I searched for a doctor, we kept trying and months were going by with no positives. I finally found a new doctor and she laid out all of the options for me. We decided to start a round of Clomid to try and help things. It was December 2018 by this point, a whole year since my second miscarriage. We were just waiting for my period to be able to start the Clomid, but it was not coming. On January 4, I was starting to get frustrated and finally decided to just take a test. I saw the faintest second line on that test and was instantly filled with fear. I struggled to feel excited because of the last two experiences. My doctor did regular bloodwork to check on my levels which started out great, but then she said they were not doubling every 72 hours as they were supposed to. But they were still going up so we just kept waiting and kept doing the bloodwork.

This pregnancy was definitely different. It was one filled with so much fear and dread of when the bleeding would start. By the end of January, I started bleeding while at work. Tears just rolled down my face. I called my doctor immediately and she brought me right in for an ultrasound. After the ultrasound she assured me it was not an ectopic pregnancy which I had feared a little after my numbers continued to rise but not double. A week later I couldn't shake the feeling that something wasn't right as I was cramping on one side and the numbers still continued to rise slowly. My doctor was out of town so another doctor urged me to go to OB Triage where they did some blood work and an ultrasound. The doctor on call came in, and I knew something was wrong. It *was* an ectopic pregnancy and I needed to go right into surgery to have it removed because my tube was starting to burst. They had to remove the pregnancy and the tube that day. I was told I would definitely have to start seeing a fertility specialist now if I hoped to get pregnant safely.

I don't think I have ever been angrier with God than I was after that loss. I was in a dark place and inside I was miserable. I felt He had taken so much from me and left me broken and alone. My husband was so good and showed me so much love and compassion during that time for which I will always be grateful. I know I couldn't have gotten through such a hard time without him there loving and supporting me every way he knew how. But it still did not stop me from hating God and pushing Him away. But the journey to become parents still was on our heart, so we sought out a fertility doctor where we got many tests done, tried our first round of Clomid and had an IUI (intrauterine insemination). To our surprise it worked and once again I had a positive pregnancy test. I had become numb by this point so there was very little joy and excitement. My mind already anticipated how this would end. And unfortunately, I was right. We lost our fourth child in July 2019. I had very little emotion to that loss. Of course, I was sad, but I had almost expected it so in a way it made it hurt a little less than the previous ones.

I cannot tell you what changed in me, but after that fourth loss something reignited in me and slowly I started drawing back to God. Talking to Him for the first time in a long time was hard. I cried and maybe even yelled at Him a bit because I still felt so broken and hurt, but I wanted to heal and work towards a better relationship with Him again. I came to a point where I realized I had been trying to do this without Him. I was trying to control this. I knew I needed to hand my dream of being a mother over to Him. I could not do it without Him anymore. Losing a child and struggling with infertility is a very lonely journey. Even when you have an army of people praying for you and there for you, you still feel so alone.

But God never gave up on me. He kept finding ways to pull me back to Him. We decided to take a break; a break to refocus on God, ourselves, and to figure out where we wanted to go from there. It was hard not trying for a whole year, but I have grown so much in that year. I've seen myself come from the darkest of places to a place where I'm just going where God leads.

This past summer we started fertility treatments again and I have learned to trust His plans and His process for us to become parents (or not become parents, because I've been learning to accept that as a possible reality as well). I have been able to step back from it all for a year and get a fresh focus on my dreams and work to line them up with God's dream and plans for me. It hasn't been an easy journey at all, but it has been *my* journey, the journey God has given me in order to grow in my faith and love for Him. And it is a beautiful journey, one that I wouldn't trade anymore for anything because it has made me, me! It has given me a unique opportunity to be a help and encouragement to others who are walking similar journeys; I have met so many amazing friends because of this journey. I have truly been able to take on the mindset of thinking I will choose to find joy in the journey God has set before me. It is a choice each person has to make, but for me it has been the best choice I could have made.

> *"For I know the plans I have for you,"*
> *declares the LORD, "plans to prosper you*
> *and not to harm you, plans to give you hope*
> *and a future."* Jeremiah 29:11

IN CLOSING...

MY DEAREST READER, I HOPE AND PRAY that this book has given you some encouragement, and pointed you to the One who offers true comfort and love in even the most difficult moments. As you contemplate all that you have just read, know that you are covered in prayer and you are not alone in this. The God of the universe loves you, and He's got this. No matter the outcome of your story, always know that God is still in control, God is still good, and God loves you. We are called to trust, not excluding the hardest seasons of life, but rather especially in the hardest seasons. There is life after loss. The depression will not last forever, but it will be an uphill fight. Find people to fight with you, to pray with you, and to carry you when you cannot stand on your own anymore. Cover your days in Scripture and prayer. In those moments when you are angry with God, pray anyways. He gets it, He understands, and He is not going anywhere. You are loved, dear friend, and the child or children that you have had to say good-bye to before you even got to hold them are loved and always will be. Hold their memory in your heart, dear Mama. Do not dwell on the pain, but rather on the grace of God that will pull you through the pain. God will turn ashes into beauty if you allow Him to. There may always be some pain in the memory of your loss, but know that it will make you stronger and God will use the hard moments of this life to conform you into the image of His Son…because dear child of God… that is the whole purpose of this life we live.

ABOUT THE AUTHOR

AMY IS A WIFE AND MOTHER FROM Buffalo, NY who has a heart that is burdened for other mothers who have experienced hardship. She currently works as the director for her church's preschool program as well as volunteers at a local crisis pregnancy center. She felt the Lord leading her to write about her struggles of having two miscarriages in order to shed the hope of God's Word to other women who have faced similar circumstances. Her goal in life is to be a godly wife and mother and to share the hope of the Gospel with everyone she meets.

CPSIA information can be obtained
at www.ICGtesting.com
Printed in the USA
BVHW081224310121
599197BV00013B/581

9 781662 805462